I0423967

POSITIVE THINKING

HOW TO ACHIEVE REAL SUCCESS & HAPPINESS IN YOUR LIFE

WITH POSITIVE THINKING, SELF-EMPOWERING AFFIRMATIONS

AND TAKING ACTION - DO IT STEVE JOBS WAY

BY

PAUL GOLEMAN

To Gabriel, Patricia and Ruben

You made this book happen. Thank you.

TABLE OF CONTENTS

INTRODUCTION

I want to thank and congratulate you for downloading the book, *"Positive Thinking: How to Achieve Real Success & Happiness in Your Life with Positive Thinking, Self-Empowering Affirmations and Taking Action - Do It Steve Jobs Way."*

The things that most people are in search of in life are real happiness and success; I believe you might not achieve these things if you lack positivity and most importantly, if you don't take the necessary actions. The journey should always begin with you putting your mind and heart to it and aligning your efforts with all your goals and dreams. Positive thinking is important in all our dealings as it makes us focused, but it is not all that you need to achieve real success and happiness. You will understand as you read through the book whose chapters have been written in a way that fully benefits you as a person.

We have the potential to make the kind of difference we want in life, and once you realize this, all areas of your life will change for the better. Whatever it is you have set out to achieve, it is of essence to equip yourself with the right tools, mentally, emotionally and physically. This should be done with the aim of making sure that you always stay on track even in the face of challenges and obstacles. Life actually becomes more meaningful if you are the kind of person who reaches out for things and opens themselves up to possibilities.

A big part of this book is meant to give you an open mind to all that is required of you to achieve great things in life. It acts on changing you from inside out and making sure you have an understanding of how things work in real life. Many of us are stuck in our comfort zones because we have allowed fear and laziness to be in full control. It is always said that you can't keep doing the same thing and expect different results. What am trying to say is that life doesn't just happen, you have to make it happen through hard work, determination, and dedication.

Every part of you play a significant role in how your life turns out to be; this includes your thoughts, feelings, actions, and habits; making it imperative for you to be keen on being in control of all aspects of your life. There is more to life than what you believe in, and this book offers you the best platform to embark on a venture of creating a more fulfilling and satisfying life.

CHAPTER ONE

POSITIVE THINKING EXPLAINED

To live a happy and progressive life all individuals need to be positive thinkers. Positive thinking is a mental attitude in which you expect great and favorable results. In other words, positive thinking is the process of creating thoughts that make and transform energy into reality. People who exercise positive thinking are those who always anticipate success, health, and happiness. They know that no matter how difficult situations are in the present or have been in the past, there will always be light at the end of the tunnel. Positive thinking is known to be effective in changing lives because it influences how you feel and the actions you take. It is meant to put you on the right track and ensures you to put efforts into making great achievements. Obviously, nothing comes easy in life, but with the right mindset, it becomes a smooth sailing journey. All one is left with is aligning the goals they have in mind with their actions.

I won't forget to mention that there is so much power in positive thinking and applying it your life along other survival skills could do you so much good. I say this because there are so many people who don't give the idea of positive thinking much credit. It has actually gained so much popularity and to effectively use it, one needs more than just the awareness of its existence but rather adopt it in all that you do. I encourage you to be a positive thinker as a way of developing a positive attitude which ultimately attracts happy and pleasant feelings. All this is necessary to our health and general wellbeing. It could be difficult to maintain positive thoughts in life due to the difficulties and challenges we experience in our day to day lives, but once you understand its worth, then you will try much to achieve it. You have nothing to lose by being more positive because negative thinking adds absolutely no value to your life.

When you think about positive thinking, it is much about your outlook on life and how you approach different things like failures, loss, etc. This kind of mindset makes it easy for you to deal with them. Positive thinking doesn't, however, mean that you bury your head in the sand and forget about all of the life's experiences and situations that are not pleasant. It is all about approaching the negative in a more productive and healthy way that ensures your general wellbeing.

It may not directly give you all you want in life, but positive thinking will create real value in your life and allow you to cultivate skills that last long. I can't say the same about negative thoughts because all they do is narrow your thinking and it makes you focus your everything on the dark side of life and could result in stress, lack of energy, lack of self-esteem, etc. In this state you tend to ignore all relevant opportunities to create solutions and progress. Generally, the worst thing about negative thoughts is that they drain you of all your energy and prevent you from living in the present. You will never notice how deep you are drowning because the more you give in to your negative thoughts the stronger they become and they will be in control of a big part of your life than you could realize.

THE MAIN BENEFITS OF POSITIVE THINKING

If there are benefits you could easily enjoy, then they are those of positive thinking, which unlike any other thing in life, they are always felt immediately. It might not be all you need in life but it is most of it. Positive thinking is believed to have a significant effect in all areas of a person's life, and its most basic is that it creates real happiness. Personally, I would give anything to be happy as it has proved to be something of real worth. Many of us are searching for other things like wealth in life, forgetting that to enjoy them fully they need to be built on the foundation of happiness. It is necessary that you get to learn about the benefits of positive thinking because it will give you more than a reason to exercise it. It gives you an idea of how your life transforms if you learn to apply it in your daily life. Explained below are the benefits of positive thinking:

• **Resilience**: Instead of you falling apart in the face of challenges and difficulties, positive thinking makes you more resilient. This is so because it will focus all your energy on the positive side of things, saving you from too much worry or sadness. The resilience will be noticed in your ability to move on with life and also overcome all kinds of obstacles.

• **Improves your health**: We all know that health conditions like stress, anxiety, and depression are as a result of negative thinking. By being a positive thinker then you reduce the risk of such conditions, and you will lead a healthier and happier life. When your mind and heart are troubled, then the chances are that your body won't function normally. Thinking positively should not be an option but rather a necessity if you want to lead a healthy life.

• **Overcome fear**: Fear can be very crippling, both mentally and emotionally as it takes over us completely. With positive thinking, an individual can conquer any kind of fear as your mind will only think of the good that should come your way.

• **Improves relationships**: A person who has positive thoughts always creates positive atmospheres and feelings. It is an essential tool in building healthy relationships as it makes you relate better with people and thus creates room for improved relationships.

- **Builds real happiness**: Another fact about thinking positively is that it makes you and the people around you happy. Hence, you will always be at peace and you will have the ability to influence the way others think and feel.

- **Increased confidence**: With positive thoughts you tend to be very comfortable in your own skin and you will appreciate your life fully. You will have the heart to face all that comes your way, as a result, you are a more confident and brave person.

CHAPTER TWO

KNOWING WHAT YOU WANT IN LIFE

The whole idea behind knowing what you want in life is so that you can find meaning and purpose. It is a chance to create awareness of who you are as a person and what you set out to achieve. If you find yourself living in circles and by that I mean working hard, but you never seem to get anywhere worthwhile, then it means you didn't take some time to determine what you want in life.

For anyone to achieve satisfaction in life, they have to focus on things that they believe complete them. You are only aware of these things if you determine the exact thing you want in life and the path you would like to follow to achieve them. This should be applicable in all areas of your life. It is impossible to work towards achieving something when you have no idea what it is you want to achieve. Finding direction is important and will make it easier for you to make your dreams a reality.

It is a challenge for many to determine what they want in life, but if you are really ambitious about making a difference then you need to work at it. Below are important ways that I believe will help you know what you want in life:

1) **Family and friends**: These are the people whom you spend a big part of your life with and could help you know what you want in life. They will advise on the things that they know you always enjoy and what they believe would be best for you depending on how well they know you.

2) **Knowledge and skills**: There are always those specific things that you are excellent at and are equipped with the required knowledge and skills to progress in life through them. This could be something you studied in school or is a talent you grew with. Going back to yourself, analyzing and searching, will help you know who you really want to be in life. This will be the beginning of a great life.

3) **Goal setting**: Another great way of knowing what you want in life is through setting goals. Have your short term and long term goals written down and they are the ones that will give you a clear idea of what you want in life. Goals have, for a long time, been known to be a source of motivation and direction and are exactly what you need.

4) **Know where your happiness**: As I said the most important thing everyone should be in search of is happiness. If you are aware of certain things that always make you happy, then you already have an answer to the question at hand. Take some time to reach deep into yourself and know the kind of things that always make you happy.

AFFIRMATIONS FOR GROWTH AND DEVELOPMENT

Affirmations are short sentences that are always believed to have a huge effect on a person's life. They normally affect the conscious and subconscious mind and their words bring up mental images that have the ability to motivate, inspire and energize. If you make it a habit of always repeating specific affirmations, then the resultant images brought about will influence a person's habits, behaviors, and actions. To achieve personal growth, it really helps to have in mind some of the best affirmations that align with your goals and dreams.

The truth is that we are what we think we are and by using affirmations you will have the power to be in full control of all your thoughts. This way you can direct them to focus on the things that are good for your general wellbeing. You, however, need to know that you can't only rely on thoughts and must work on transforming those thoughts into words and ultimately into actions.

The best thing is that the moment you affirm your dreams and desires you will be empowered with a sense of reassurance that your words will become your reality. The thing is, when you think of all your desires - your thoughts will create your reality. Explained below are important affirmations for your personal development that I believe will be of so much help:

MY FAILURES ARE A LEARNING EXPERIENCE

Affirming to this every day gives you a different approach towards failure and helps you know that failure does not mean you are not good enough. The most successful individuals are those who understand that it is through failure that we grow and also through failure that we achieve great things.

I CREATE VALUE IN MY OWN LIFE

This reminds you of your responsibility to always make yourself better in all ways and focus your efforts on doing things that only add value to all areas of your life.

I HAVE WHAT IT TAKES TO BE A SUCCESS

The truth is that we all have so much potential within us to achieve greatness, but if you lack this awareness, then you won't go far in life. As a person, it really helps to remind yourself every day that you actually have what it takes, and you will never give up on your dreams.

I APPRECIATE MYSELF AND WHERE I AM IN LIFE

It is through self-love and appreciation that individuals can attain real success and happiness in life. This, therefore, means that self-appreciation makes you view the world differently and will help you approach life with more confidence and bravery.

I AM VERY HARD WORKING

Apart from positive thinking, hard work comes in as a major factor in achieving goals and dreams. It is therefore very essential to remind yourself every day how hard working you are, and you will end up being exactly that.

My life is changing for the better

This affirmation is meant to help you be the kind of person who embraces change and does not allow any challenges or obstacles deter them from growing. It is also helpful in giving you the realization that your life is changing and that you are doing good work on that.

CHAPTER THREE

HABITS FOR SUCCESSFUL PEOPLE

People who have highly succeeded in life have so many things in common, and this is seen in their way of doing things or rather habits. If you want to put yourself in line with your goals, then it could really help to be aware of such practices. They will open your mind to the small things you should do that could actually have a big effect on your life. By introducing them to your lifestyle, you will ultimately increase productivity. One should know that habits can either help or hurt you depending on which ones you decide to uphold. Bad habits take you away from the things you want to do, whereas good habits bring you closer by helping you build a life full of accomplishments and action.

You got nothing to lose but so much to gain if you practice some of the specific habits successful people have. What they do is change your way of thinking and of doing things ensuring that they are all in line with your ambitions. Success is not limited to specific individuals as some learnable behaviors can make success more achievable. You will be surprised to find that they are simple things that won't take much of your energy to follow and are as explained below:

1) **Manage emotions**: One great thing about successful people is that they always try really hard to be in control of their emotions by not allowing certain situations or experiences determine how they act. They are always ready to look above the negativity and find better things to focus their thoughts and feelings on. In times of failures they are ready to find better strategies and they don't let failures be the reason for their downfall.

2) **Wake up early**: Waking up early is an effective habit to follow, and successful people understand this. They know that early wakers tend to be optimistic and energetic. By getting up early in the morning, one tends to be more energetic throughout the day and will, therefore, handle so much more thus increasing their productivity.

3) **Visualize**: Visualization is much about picturing in your mind all your goals and dreams and it is something most successful people do. It acts as a source of motivation and makes you believe in your goals and dreams. By visualizing these things, a big part of you embraces the idea, and all your efforts will naturally be aligned with your desires.

4) **Planning:** It is impossible to achieve much in life if you lack a plan and this is the reason why entrepreneurs always plan before they act. Through planning, one will have an idea on how to effectively distribute their resources and the specific actions that should be taken. Planning ahead gives

you a rough idea of all that is required of you and what your expectations should be.

5) **Optimism**: This is all about having positive thoughts and feelings and it's much of what you need to create the life you desire. The thing is that optimistic people are always ready to make sacrifices or take risks and never allow any obstacle to deter them from reaching their goals. Both their heart and mind cooperate in proving that nothing is impossible to achieve and are therefore very progressive.

6) **Prioritize**: Another common thing about many people who have ended up being successful is that they have priorities. They handle the important things which are believed to be more efficient first and the rest later. Through this they are also able to avoid procrastination which is actually a killer of dreams.

7) **Work hard**: You can't get anywhere in life if you just sit around and do nothing. Life is all about creating, and you only do this when you work hard and learn to make sacrifices. It is through efforts that you will get to the point you want to be in life as nothing happens on its own.

CHAPTER FOUR

MORE TO SUCCESS THAN HAVING POSITIVE THOUGHTS

Am sure you already understand the importance of being a positive thinker and the difference it can make in your life. One thing about thinking positively is that it puts you on the right track, and actually, to make your journey purposeful, you have to put in efforts. It is said that the harder you work the luckier you become which is very true because nothing in life just happens. To be the best athlete in your chosen sport you have to practice real hard, to get good grades you have to read hard and this is just what life is all about.

If it was all about sitting down and waiting for things to happen through manifestation, then nothing will be of value. You have to sweat for you to achieve real success, and this is what makes life interesting. Many people read about positive thinking and believe it all ends there; I want to enlighten you today and assure you that it is through actions that change happens. Begin your journey to greatness by knowing what you want, believing in your ability to achieve and then more importantly work towards achieving.

A good thing about positive thinking is that it creates a progressive attitude as it brings in determination and self-belief. You will have no doubts in the mind of being the person you want and will, therefore, put in your all to ensure that it actually happens. Once you are in the mood to work, then it will all be enjoyable and won't seem like so much of a task. It is said that the mind is so powerful, as it could turn you into a success or a loser. We say that what you think is what you become because when you think positively then it is the positive path you are likely to follow.

When I talk about working hard and putting more effort, I mean reaching out to the world and creating your own opportunities. Don't wait for the world to deliver, but instead, make it deliver! Have an open mind in all that you do and be the kind of person who looks for solutions instead of giving up when things don't work your way. This could entail increasing your knowledge and skills and so much more as a way of making yourself better.

According to the law of 'cause and effect', nothing in life happens by chance and all your actions have reactions. It says that all our words, thoughts, and actions are causes that send off a wave of energy into the universe which will, in turn, create an effect that could either be desirable or not. Good thoughts and actions are therefore considered to be essential for a great and better life.

If you want to be successful, then all your thoughts and actions should demonstrate the same. What I am trying to say is that to lead a happy and successful life you need to believe in its possibility and then work towards making that your reality. The law of 'cause and effect' is trying to teach you that there is more to life than just thinking positively and that so much more is required of you to achieve all your goals.

DO IT STEVE JOBS' WAY

Am sure you may have heard about Steve Jobs and would probably want to be like him in various ways. I say this because apart from being wealthy, he instilled in me a concept that has for a long time been a part of me. Who he was and the story he created provides a continuous source of motivation to many. There is so much to his name that I believe is worth my recognition as I try to instill in your mind the idea of positive thinking and effort. So how exactly do you know him?

Steve jobs is described as the most innovative business person who revolutionized computing, telephony, retailing, etc. He was the man behind the Apple Company. His success is known to have been made possible by him being more focused and determined on what was to be achieved. In his journey to make the significant achievements, he encountered all kinds of pitfalls and challenges, but he only focused on the goals he had in mind.

Looking deep into his professional life and accomplishments, Steve Jobs displays unique qualities that if many adopted the world would be a different place. His whole life is seen to have been one with a lot of challenges, but he overlooked all that and built a great and meaningful life. These include things like the fact that he was adopted after birth, he dropped out of college and was a real struggle for him to survive as he unofficially attended classes, his GPA was very low, and he never enjoyed school structure, etc.

What I am trying to bring out is that once you feel like there is something you really have to achieve in life then you should go for it. Don't allow your circumstances or thoughts to prevent you from taking the first step. As I already mentioned, in life you need to really struggle or rather, work extremely hard for you to progress. If Steve Jobs didn't look beyond who he was and tried to make something of himself, then so much would not have been created in his name. Having determined your purpose or what you think is suitable for you then nothing should stop you from acting on that. Steve jobs life is worth recognizing because of his great achievements and that has made a difference in many people's lives.

CHAPTER FIVE

EFFECTIVE STEPS TO BUILD A LIFE OF REAL SUCCESS AND HAPPINESS

We all have our own definition of success, but whatever yours is I hope that it is molded with happiness. Society defines success based on material things and is the reason why so many people are living miserably. Others lack their own definition of success and are striving to be successful under the conditions and terms of other people. This is the reason why you feel that your life lacks satisfaction and fulfillment. There is no specific definition of the word success that suits everyone because it means differently to different people. To some, success is all about making a difference in the life of one person and to others it means having so much money or a very big house. To be truly successful you need to attain all of its elements, which include happiness, health, and wealth.

Anyone can start today and be really successful, no matter how terrible your current situation seems. All you have to do is make that decision and start working towards that specific goal. This part of the book will enlighten you on the specific steps you need to take for you to be both successful and happy. It will open you up to the reality of how the world works, giving you an idea on where to focus your energy and efforts. Regardless of your age, gender, family background, current situation or even level of education, you can do so much to achieve so much in life.

SELF-EVALUATION

Before one embarks on a journey of creating success and happiness they need to begin by reaching into their inner self and find out what they want in life and how far they can go to be that. As you evaluate yourself, you will have a chance to have your goals in mind and find out what will be required of you to be great.

GOAL SETTING

It is crucial to have goals in life as they provide you with direction. They will always allow you to put your heart and mind into the things you want to attain. When setting goals, make sure that they are smart, measurable, accurate, realistic and time bound. Have both long-term and short-term goals so that you will do things a step at a time. Life is about taking things a step at a time and allowing the smaller goals lead you to bigger ones. As you strive to build your desired kind of life, goals will put you on track and you will know how to allocate resources.

TIME MANAGEMENT

You should know that time is an imperative aspect of our lives and once lost cannot be recovered. To ensure that you are able to do so much then it is important that you delegate and manage your time effectively. This is a good way to make sure that you lead a less stressful life and also a productive one. With a good time management, one is able to put in place all that is on their agenda and thus will be in a better position to be successful.

FOCUS

Being focused is about being keen and in touch with all that you do in life and it is a good way of achieving success. There are so many distractions in life, including the challenges we face, but with a focused mind, you will never move away from your targets. A focused person is always willing to sacrifice both time and energy in order to change all areas of their life. They don't give in to pressure or demands but rather fight back when things seem difficult.

BELIEVE IN YOURSELF

Self-belief is considered as an essential tool in making life better and successful. Many of us allow their experiences and challenges to hold us back, but with self-belief then you have the heart to conquer all. Self-believe is all about appreciating who you are and trusting in all your abilities. With this kind of living, so much success and happiness will come your way.

LIVING IN THE MOMENT

Instead of worrying about the future or regretting about the past, you can be more productive if you learn to focus on the present. When you learn to be aware of the present moment, it will be easier for you to progress in life. You will know how to invest your resources now so that you can create a brighter future.

GROW YOUR KNOWLEDGE AND SKILLS

You are only able to stand out and achieve better things in life if you make an effort in improving your knowledge and skills. This is so because you will handle all tasks and challenges that you are presented with and create more possibilities. The world is evolving and so should you; learn new things so that you can be more innovative.

CONCLUSION

It is my hope that this book was able to give you an understanding of what is required of you to build a successful and happy life. Its focus was on making you know that as much as positive thinking could point you in the right direction; it is not enough to help reach your goals. There is more to life that people need to know if it is in their desire to change their destiny. It is, therefore, your responsibility to put into practice all that you have learnt for you to appreciate this book.

ABOUT THE AUTHOR

Hi, I'm Paul and here's a little about me:

I'm an entrepreneur, internet marketer, author, life coach, professional speaker, fitness enthusiast, and world traveler. I feel extremely blessed for the life that I live.

I bring 7 years of niche expertise in self-help and personal development. I'm a business management graduate and I like to study people who appear to be unbeatable against all oddities or challenges of life. I seek answers for failures, lack of growth and thus I want to help people reinvent themselves. I believe: Each and every person is the sole controller of his/her life. If you do not take an utmost care of your life, no one else will.

PREVIEW OF: CONFIDENCE

MY PERSONAL GUIDE TO BUILDING SELF-CONFIDENCE THAT WILL DESTROY YOUR SHYNESS, BOOST YOUR SELF-ESTEEM & HELP YOU ACHIEVE YOUR GOALS

INTRODUCTION

As you probably already know, self-confidence is necessary if you want to fulfill your potential. If you have anything less than extreme confidence, then you have at least some doubts about yourself and your abilities. It is completely normal to have self-doubt, but I don't want you to settle for "normal". Greatness is your aim from now on, and I am going to give you a formula that you can use to achieve it.

In essence, confidence can be boiled down to one thing: self-love. You must first feel that you are worthy of what you want. To feel worthy, you must come face to face with your deepest fears and insecurities because when you finally bring them to the light, they will vanish, bringing you a sense of confidence and peace of mind that you've never felt before. Extreme confidence is possible for you, no matter where you are starting from. Let's find out what it's going to take, shall we?

CHAPTER 1:

WHAT IS SELF-CONFIDENCE?

The nature of life is that it sometimes throws us a curve ball. Not everything works out as expected, and we can begin to question numerous parts of our own mind... This can be true of any number of areas of life, from our finances to our spiritual health, or the state of our relationships with others. But the abiding thread that links them all is our sense of self-worth and self-confidence.

If life somewhat resembles a rollercoaster, then self-confidence is the ability to realize that the rollercoaster will come to an end and that the highs on the journey are just as disingenuous as the lows.

Knowledge of that fact doesn't necessarily help when you happen to be at the low end of the spectrum! But it is nevertheless useful to reflect on moments in your life and realize that it is only when things are going badly that most of us start to doubt ourselves, and wonder if we will ever see the sunset again.

In addition to viewing self-confidence as an amalgam of the rich tapestry of life's experience, it can also be viewed in the context of a minute by minute assessment of how we view ourselves.

This tends to come into play with such issues as body image, and in this regard, there are more differences between the sexes.

Men most certainly do suffer from body image at times, and it would be a rare man who said that they haven't at times looked at parts of their body and wished them different. But the fact remains that whilst men do harbour thoughts about ways that they would like to improve themselves (six-pack abs please!), there are perhaps greater issues of self-confidence over body image when it comes to women.

There are probably sound biological reasons for this in all honesty, in addition to the much trotted out "media influence"; because the fact remains that men tend to be unduly influenced (at least at first, we get deeper later!) by how a woman looks. And women are certainly not blind to that fact, so certainly in young women, there is always a pressure to look good so that they will find more success with men, and that inevitably plays into the whole question of self-confidence.

Perhaps it can be said that if someone had perfect self-confidence, they would occupy some island, looking out contentedly at others, but not unduly concerned by their opinion. But we know that in reality no such person exists, and hence that self-confidence is an issue for all of us.

And then, of course, there genuinely is the "media influence" that projects images of ultra-skinny girls on to the consciousness's of women and does make them question their appearance.

Self-confidence is an issue that like the clouds is hard to pin down, but is all around us.

CHAPTER 2:

SELF CONFIDENCE AT THE OFFICE

There are a lot of individuals in this world who feel very confident in their regular life, but for some reason, they just cannot experience that same confidence in the workplace. If you are one of these people, then you're going to need to learn how to improve self-esteem at the workplace so that this doesn't become the main issue for you any longer. I have some really good tips that should help you improve in these areas if you take the time to put them into practice and incorporate them into your daily routine.

The first tip for enhancing your confidence at the office is to begin accepting projects that you would normally reject out of fear. The primary way you're going to improve your confidence at work is by facing your fears, and the only way you're going to face your fears is if you begin to work on the things that make you afraid. So, accept those extra projects and make it a point to do your best and your confidence will grow no matter what.

The second idea for improving your self-confidence at the workplace is to expand your skill set so that you can become a greater asset to your company. The one thing your company demands out of all of its employees is people who take their business seriously and people who are willing to go the extra mile to improve their position. This is an instant confidence booster, and it is also going to help you make a lot more money in the end, so it's win-win all around.

The third confidence boosting tip I'd like to give you is....

To check out the rest of this book search it on amazon as "Confidence Paul Goleman"

Or go here for more books by Paul Goleman:

http://www.amazon.com/Paul-Goleman/e/B01EPDLLLO

ONE LAST THING...

If you enjoyed this book or found it useful I'd be very grateful if you'd post a short review on Amazon. Your support really does make a difference and I read all the reviews personally so I can get your feedback and make this book even better.

Thanks again for your support!

www.ingramcontent.com/pod-product-compliance
Lightning Source LLC
Chambersburg PA
CBHW061931280526
45787CB00004B/1567